Steps in Life – YOUR Life

Steps in Life – YOUR Life

By
James M. Cain

E-BookTime, LLC
Montgomery, Alabama

Steps in Life – YOUR Life

Library of Congress Control Number: 2011918350

ISBN: 978-1-60862-340-2

First Edition
Published October 2011
E-BookTime, LLC
6598 Pumpkin Road
Montgomery, AL 36108
www.e-booktime.com

I dedicate this book to my daughter Celia Allison who encouraged me to continue working on it until it was finished.

Introduction

This booklet was designed and written to make your steps in life easier. Your steps in life can be traced by the records you make during your lifetime. This booklet provides you with specific information on how to accomplish some very important aspects of your life. (See Contents for subjects covered.)

I started my research on this booklet when I was seventy-five years young. I figured by this age that I had done enough research and gained enough knowledge to write down the steps of life.

Steps in life begin with a slap on the backside. This is step one; the Birth Certificate is made. The second step is obtaining a Social Security number and the records of life begin. As I said before, records are very important; we cannot live without them. Once the Birth Certificate and Social Security number has been established, you are on your way.

A Birth Certificate is needed to obtain a Social Security number, which in turn is used to enter school, obtain a passport, a drivers' license, and many other Federal and State requirements.

To help you understand just how important records are, let me tell you a little story about what happened to my friends' family in 1981. My friends' father died and he did not keep any record of where he kept important papers. The father kept everything to himself and the mother did not know anything and never asked. It took the family about three months to get all the important papers together. The reason it took so long is because the family did not have any knowledge of where all the important papers were: like the insurance policy, the will, military papers, marriage license, income tax records, vehicle title, property deed, and more.

The family could not collect the fathers' insurance because they did not have his Birth Certificate, Marriage License, and a certified copy of the Death Certificate.

These are only a few of the problems that developed because a record or list of important documents and their storage location was not maintained and up-dated as necessary. It is imperative that your important records and papers be kept updated and stored in a safe place.

REMEMBER – Without records, you have not lived!

Life Management Skills

Analyzing
Appraising
Categorizing
Communicating
Computer Skills
Conferring/Conferencing
Counseling
Estimating
Evaluating
Following Directions
Interviewing
Investigating
Listening
Negotiating
Perceiving
Persuading
Planning
Predicting
Presenting
Prioritizing
Reading
Self-Assessment
Setting Goals
Speaking
Summarizing
Synthesizing
Teaching
Teaming with Others
Time Management
Writing

Learn, spell, and know the meaning of these words and you will go far.

Personal Affairs Questions

If you answer "No" or "I don't know" to any of the questions listed below, educate yourself – FAST.

1. Do you have important papers and records available in case you need them in a hurry? Where are the papers kept?

2. Do you know your net worth?

3. Do you or your spouse have a will? Where is the will kept?

4. Do you operate on a budget? How much do you spend each month? How much do you need to live on each month?

5. Do you have an inventory of your personal assets? How much are your personal assets worth?

6. Do you have children? Has someone been appointed as a guardian in case of death of both parents? Does the appointed guardian know that they are in the will?

7. Do you have a safe deposit box? Does someone know where the box is located? What is the safe

deposit box number? Where is the key to safe deposit box?

8. Do you have a bank/Credit Union checking account? What is the name of the bank or Credit Union? What is the account number? Whose name is on the account?

9. Do you have a bank/Credit Union savings account? What is the name of the bank/Credit Union? What is the account number? Whose name is on the account?

10. Do you or your spouse have an Individual Retirement Account (IRA)? What firm/organization handles the account? What name is on the account? What is the IRA account number?

11. Do you own any U.S. Government Saving Bonds? Where are the Bonds kept? Have you written down the serial numbers from the bonds in case of loss?

12. Do you have life insurance policies? What is the insurance company's name? What are the policy account numbers? Who is the beneficiary of the policy? What is the amount of the policy?

13. Where are your Income Tax Returns kept?

14. Is your car title in both of your names? Where is the car title(s) kept?

15. Is the deed to your property in both of your names? Where is the property deed kept?

16. Do you have mortgage insurance on your home? What insurance company handles the mortgage insurance?

17. Where do you want to be buried? Do you want to be buried or cremated? Do you want a Military Honors funeral? Do you want a government headstone for your grave site?

18. Where do you get emergency cash when your spouse is out of town?

19. Do you have an individual credit rating or do you use your spouse's?

20. Do you have medical insurance in case of a serious illness in the family?

Note: Most of these questions can be answered by completing the Personal Affairs Data Worksheet (see next page). The Personal Affairs Data Worksheet can be changed as often as necessary to meet your changing needs.

Personal Affairs Data Worksheet

Date_____________ Family Name_________________

1. Your Name____________________________
2. Your Date of Birth______________________
3. Place of Birth__________________________
4. Social Security Number__________________

5. Spouse Name________________________
6. Date of Birth__________________________
7. Place of Birth_________________________
8. Social Security Number________________

9. Home Address______________________

____

10. Home Tele_________________________
11. Cell Phone_________________________

Employment

12. Name of Employer__________________
13. Address___________________________

____

14. Telephone_________________________

15. Name of Employer__________________
16. Address___________________________

____

17. Telephone_________________________

18. Employer______________________________
19. Address________________________________

____

20. Telephone______________________________

21. Employer______________________________
22. Address________________________________

____

23. Telephone______________________________

Attorney

24. Attorney Name________________________
25. Address________________________________

____

26. Telephone______________________________

Health Insurance Information/Doctors

27. Company Name_______________________
28. Policy Number________________________

29. Doctor's Name________________________
30. Address________________________________

____

31. Telephone______________________________

32. Doctor's Name________________________
33. Address________________________________

____

34. Telephone______________________________

35. Dentist Name________________________
36. Address_____________________________
____
37. Telephone___________________________

Drivers' License Information
38. Your Drivers' License Number__________________
39. Spouse Drivers' License Number_______________

Vehicle Information
40. Year________________________________
41. Make_______________________________
42. Model______________________________
43. VIN Number_________________________
44. Color_______________________________
45. Tag Number_________________________

46. Year________________________________
47. Make_______________________________
48. Model______________________________
49. VIN Number_________________________
50. Color_______________________________
51. Tag Number_________________________

Bank Information
52. Name of Bank______________________________
Address_______________________________________
Tele number___________________________________
53. Account Number Checking___________________
54. Account Number Savings____________________

55. Name of Bank______________________________
Address______________________________________
Tele number__________________________________
56. Account Number Checking___________________
57. Account Number Savings____________________

Credit Union Information

58. Credit Union Name__________________________
Address______________________________________
Tele number__________________________________
59. Account Number Checking___________________
60. Account Number Savings____________________

U.S. Government Saving Bonds

61. Year Purchased_______Value_______________
Serial Number________________________________
62. Year Purchased_______Value_______________
Serial Number________________________________
63. Year Purchased_______Value_______________
Serial Number________________________________
64. Year Purchased_______Value_______________
Serial Number________________________________
65. Year Purchased________Value______________
Serial Number________________________________
66. Year Purchased________Value______________
Serial Number________________________________
67. Year Purchased________Value______________
Serial Number________________________________
68. Year Purchased________Value______________
Serial Number________________________________

69. Year Purchased________Value______________
Serial Number________________________________
70. Year Purchased________Value______________
Serial Number________________________________
71. Year Purchased________Value______________
Serial Number________________________________
72. Year Purchased________Value______________
Serial Number________________________________
73. Year Purchased________Value______________
Serial Number________________________________
74. Year Purchased________Value______________
Serial Number________________________________
75. Year Purchased________Value______________
Serial Number________________________________

Note: You can add as many as you like by adding another blank page

Retirement Accounts

76. Name of IRA_________________________
Address________________________________
Tele number____________________________
Account number_________________________

77. Name of IRA_________________________
Address________________________________
Tele number____________________________
Account number_________________________

Credit Card Information

78. Company Name____________________________
Account Number______________________________
Phone Number________________________________

79. Company Name____________________________
Account Number______________________________
Phone Number________________________________

80. Company Name____________________________
Account Number______________________________
Phone Number________________________________

Property Owned

81. Address__________________________________
____
Date of Purchase______________________________

Other Property Owned

82. Address__________________________________
____
Date of Purchase______________________________

Personal Affairs Master Records Checklist

- o Will
- o Life Insurance Policies
- o Home Insurance Policy
- o Health Insurance Policy
- o Automobile Titles
- o Property Titles (Real Estate)
- o Bank Checking Account
- o Bank/Credit Union Savings Account
- o Marriage License
- o Divorce Certificate
- o Military Records (DD form 214's)
- o School Records
- o Birth Certificates
- o Social Security Account Record
- o Credit Card Numbers Record
- o Safety Deposit Box (location)
- o Federal/State Income Tax Records
- o Personal Property Tax Records
- o U.S Government Saving Bonds (serial numbers recorded)
- o Mutual Funds, Stocks, CD's (location)
- o List of Creditors
- o List of Debtors
- o Inventory of Personal Property
- o Automobile Tag Numbers (recorded)
- o Family Immunization Records
- o Passports (serial numbers recorded)
- o IRA Account Numbers (location)

Personal Affairs Records Disposition

Where to Store – When to Destroy

Document	Where to Keep	When to Destroy
Check Register	Home File	Hold One Year
Cancelled Checks	Home File	Hold One Year/Hold Seven if Supports Tax Filings
Check Statement	Home File	Hold One Year
Educational Records	Home File	Give to Children When They Move
Mortgage Papers	Fire Resistant Box	Keep Three Years After Mortgage is Paid Off
Veterinary Records	Home File	Keep as Long as You Own Pet
Telephone, Cable, Electric, Water, Gas, Internet	Home File	Hold 45 Days after Payment
Birth Certificate		Indefinitely
Marriage License		Indefinitely

Document	Where to Keep	When to Destroy
Divorce Decree		Indefinitely
Citizenship Papers		Indefinitely
Military Records		Indefinitely
Will		Indefinitely
Living Will		Indefinitely
Vehicle Titles		Until Sold
Power of Attorney	Fire Resistant Box	Until Up-Dated
Car Insurance		Until Updated
Life Insurance		Keep While in Force
Home Insurance		Keep While in Force
Passports		Indefinitely
Federal Tax Records		Keep for 7 years

Financial Management

Financial management begins when you know what you own and what you owe. This can be accomplished by completing a financial statement. The financial statement reflects your assets and liabilities. When the statement is complete you will know your net worth.

A financial statement worksheet is attached for your use. The worksheet can be changed to meet your needs.

Family Budget Suggestions

- Establish Realistic Goals.
- Set Your Financial Goals.
- Determine What You Spend and Where it Goes.
- Know What Your Income Is and Where it Comes From.
- Set Up a Budget Plan That Will Help You Accomplish Your Goals.
- Set Aside Savings for Retirement.
- Establish a "Rainey Day Fund" for Emergencies (important)
- Give Each Family Member a Personal Allowance.
- Keep Debts Within Reason.
- Keep Your Budget Flexible as Life and Situations Change.

Note: Make changes as necessary to accomplish your goals!

How to Prepare a Budget

Your Budget – Where to Start

The best place to start is to do the hardest part first, that is getting together all the necessary information to determine where you spent your money in the last 12 months. In today's market and society, most people live month to month, but in order to have a strong and realistic budget, you have to start with a 12 month history of your typical spending habits.

Information needed:

Pay Slips
Bank Deposits
Rent/Mortgage Receipts
Cancelled Checks
Auto Gas Receipts
Home Repair Receipts
Auto Repair Receipts
Utility Receipts
Medical/Dental Receipts
Grocery Receipts

All the above information is essential in preparing a good budget, so please take your time so you do not forget something important. Now that you have all the necessary information, you can start working on your budget. Your budget can be changed as necessary to meet your requirements and goals. A worksheet follows for your convenience.

Budget Worksheet

Monthly Expenses

Rent/Mortgage $________
Food $________
Utilities $________
Gas
Water
Electric
Telephone/Cell
Cable
Trash Pick-up
Internet
Savings $________
School Lunches $________
Laundry $________
Child Care $________
Entertainment $________
Other/Misc $________
Total $______________

Yearly Expenses

House Insurance $________
Car Insurance $________
Life Insurance $________
Property Tax $________
Auto Tags $________
Auto Inspection $________
Post Office Box $________
Total $____________

Non-Recurring Expenses

Medical Bills $________
Dental Bills $________
Glasses/Contacts $________
Subscriptions $________
Dues $________
Gifts $________
Auto Repairs $________
Total $___________

Total Annual Expenses

Multiply monthly expenses by 12 $____________
Yearly Expenses $____________
Non-Recurring Expenses $____________
Total $________________

Personal Income

Annual Income $____________
Interest Earned $____________
Other Income $____________
Total $________________

Total Income $____________
Subtract Expenses $ -___________
Balance $________________

Cash Flow Statement

Family Name ______________________ Date ___________

Income	Yours	Hers	Total
Salary/Wages	________	________	________
Social Security	________	________	________
Retirement	________	________	________
Int/Dividends	________	________	________
Sale of Property	________	________	________
Misc Income	________	________	________
		Total $	____________

Expenses			
Savings	________	________	________
Income Taxes	________	________	________
Telephone	________	________	________
Property Taxes (Family)			________
Property Insurance (Family)			________
Vehicle Insurance (Family)			________
Misc Expense (Family)			________
Electric (Family)			________
Water Family			________
Garbage Family			________

(Continue next page)

Family Name ____________________ Date __________

Expenses (continued)

	Yours	Hers	Total
Mortgage Family			_______
Home Repair			_______
Food Family			_______
Vehicle Gas	_______	_______	_______
Eat Out Family	_______	_______	_______
Vacation Family			_______
Clothing Family			_______
School Lunches			_______
Kids' Allowance			_______
Mom's Allowance			_______
Dad's Allowance			_______
Misc Cost	_______	_______	_______

Total Expense ___________

Total Income ___________
Minus Expense ___________
Cash on Hand ___________

Assets and Liabilities

Check – List

Assets

- Cash in your pocket.
- Money you have in your checking account.
- Money you have in your savings account.
- Money you have in your Credit Union.
- Money you can get if you cashed in your Life Insurance Policy.
- Money you can get from your Invested Retirement Fund.
- Cash value of your U.S. Government Savings Bonds if you cashed them in today.
- Current market value of your home and property if it were sold today.
- Current market value of your furniture and appliances if they were sold today.
- Current market value of all your personal property items: clothing, jewelry, coin collection, antiques, etc.
- Money people owe you and you can back.
- All other goods/assets that could be sold that are not previously listed.

Liabilities

- Amount owed on your home and property.
- Amount owed on your furniture, TV, appliances, tools, etc.
- Amount owed on all vehicles, boats, trailers, etc.
- Amount owed on your charge accounts.
- Amount owed on your credit cards.
- Amount owed to family, friends and/or buddies.
- Amount owed for all other goods and services not previously listed.

Net Worth Balance Sheet

Family Name ____________________ Date _________

Assets

Cash on Hand ______________
US Gov Bonds ______________
Checking Acct ______________
Savings Acct ______________
IRA Acct ______________
Home Value ______________
Auto Value ______________
All Other Vehicles ______________
Household Property Value ______________
Coin Collection Value ______________
Stamp Collection Value ______________
Tools ______________
Antiques ______________
All Other Assets ______________

Total Assets ____________________

Net Worth Balance Sheet
(Continued)

Liabilities

Home Mortgage ________________
Auto Loans ________________
Credit Cards Debt ________________
Any Other Debt ________________

Total Liabilities ______________________

Total Assets ______________________
Minus Liabilities ______________________

Net Worth ______________________

Notes

Notes

Credit Use

Credit is good if used properly. Good credit is needed if you wish to buy a home, vehicles, appliances, or other items. Good credit is obtained by paying off credit balances on time and in full. If you are late paying balances every month, it goes on your credit history. If you pay off a balance early, that also goes on your credit history.

If you have been turned down for credit recently, you are eligible for a free copy of your credit report. This report will contain all credit purchases and their balance(s). The report will also give a credit score on how well you paid on your credit balances. The credit scores will be added up for a total credit score. The score is a three digit number based on all credit and credit applications. A copy of your credit report can be obtained by calling one or all three major credit reporting agencies:

EXPERIAN (formerly known as TRW) 1-888-397-3742
TRANSUNION CORP 1-800-916-8800
EQUIFAX 1-800-846-5279

Note: It is best to order a copy from each agency, as they may differ slightly.

If you feel that an item listed on your report is wrong, the reporting agency must remove the item unless the creditor verifies that the information is correct. Reporting agencies cannot charge more than $10.00 for a copy of your report. The Federal Trade Commission will however adjust this fee annually based on inflation. Some states have lower fees.

Credit Cards

Your life with Credit Cards can be good IF you know your limitations. To determine IF you know your limitations, answer the following questions.

1. Are you able to pay all your bills each month?

2. Do you often charge small items (under $15.00) because you do not have the cash/money available?

3. Do you write POST-DATED checks because you are out of money before payday?

4. Do you borrow money to pay a past-due bill?

5. Have you received three or more late payment warnings in the last 12 months?

6. Do you fall behind on your monthly utility bills?

7. Do you pay your rent/mortgage past the due date, thereby charged a penalty?

8. Do you worry about your un-paid debts?

IF you answered yes to three or more of these questions, you are a problem borrower and need some financial counseling/guidance.

Credit Card Control

1. Limit the number of Credit Cards you carry at one time. (If you do not carry it, then you cannot use it.)

2. Apply for Credit Cards that have no annual fee. (You save money.)

3. Apply for Credit Cards that carry a GRACE period of 25-30 days. (You save money if it is paid in full or at least the last few purchases.)

4. Keep all Credit Card receipts until you receive your monthly statement, reconcile statement with receipts, and then shred.

5. Keep a list of all your Credit Cards in a safe place. (This is handy if one is lost or stolen.)

6. Watch your Credit Card at all times while it is in the hands of store clerks or other places of business. (This cuts down on identity theft, fraud, and unauthorized use.)

7. Destroy all carbon copies after signing the receipt.

8. Never give out your Credit Card number over the phone unless you have initiated the call.

9. Carry a Credit Card only if you are going to use it.

Good Advice: Only have one Credit Card for all purchases!

Credit Card Errors

Credit Card billing errors do occur, so here are a few pointers in resolving problems that may occur.

1. Under the Fair Credit Billing Act, you must send the creditor a written notice about the billing error to avoid paying for any disputed charges. Many consumers do not know this!

2. To be protected under the Fair Billing Act, here is what you need to do:

   a. Write the bank or retailer who issued the card. Your letter must be received within 60 days after the bill containing the errors was mailed. In your letter, include your name, account number, the date and dollar amount of the charges you are contesting, and why you think there was an error.

   b. Make sure you send the letter to the right office address. To determine the proper address, look at your statement and then find the heading "Send Inquiries To."

   c. Do not put your letter in the same envelope as your payment.

d. To make absolutely sure that the creditor receives your letter, you may wish to send the letter by certified mail.

3. If you follow the instructions above, then the creditor are required to:

   a. Acknowledge your letter in writing within 30 days after they receive it, unless the problem is corrected/resolved within that time.

   b. Conduct a reasonable investigation and within 90 days, either explain why the bill is correct or correct the error.

   c. If you ask for "Proof" in your letter and the creditor states that the bill is correct, then the creditor must provide documents showing that the charges were correct.

Note: If you need more information about the law and the Fair Credit Billing Act, you may contact the "Federal Trade Commission" for a FREE brochure. You may also locate the Federal Trade Commission on the internet.

Federal Trade Commission
600 Pennsylvania Ave. NW
Washington, DC 20580

www.ftc.gov

Identification Theft

Identity theft is a serious problem-it happens when a thief pretends to be you and uses your personal information when applying for credit cards, bank loans, and can go as far as creating Birth Certificates and drivers' license in your name. A thief can get your personal information from the following sources:

1. Your lost or stolen wallet.

2. Stealing your mail out of your mailbox or your trash.

3. Discarded credit card receipts.

4. Going through your trash.

5. Hacking into your computer files.

6. Watching you while you are in the check out line for your PIN.

Protect yourself from identification theft by:

1. Leave your social security card at home unless you need it for a specific purpose.

2. Never carry credit cards that you do not need.

3. Never carry your passport unless you intend to travel outside the country.

4. Never carry your Birth Certificate unless it is needed for a specific purpose.

5. Never give out your social security number before asking why it is needed. Only your employer should have your social security number for tax purposes. Other places of business that may need it is a bank to open an account or other business to verify your credit history when applying for credit.

6. For all practical purposes, shred all unwanted documents, including mail.

Retirement Planning

Retirement planning MUST start in your young years. If you start planning at age twenty-one, you will have forty-five years to save your retirement nest-egg. If you hit the Lottery, you may be able to retire early, but do not count on it!

If you start saving twenty-five dollars per month – you save $300 per year and in forty-five years that becomes $13,500 plus interest. If you save fifty dollars a month – you save $600 per year and in forty-five years your savings will be $27,000 plus interest. If you save one hundred dollars per month – you save $1,200 a year and in forty-five years, your savings will be $54,000 plus interest.

It does not really matter how much you save, only that you start saving today! Every little bit counts towards your day of retirement.

Tips on saving:

1. You may start out your savings plan by buying US Government Savings Bond per month. If you buy a $50 Savings Bond, you will pay $25 for the Bond and in thirty years (date of maturity) if will be worth $50. This is an excellent way to start saving.

Note: After the maturity date, the bond will not accrue any more interest.

2. Another way to save is to put loose change in a cookie jar.

3. Do not spend money you do not have. Live within your means/budget.

4. Make a budget plan and stick to it; make sure you pay yourself first.

As part of your retirement planning – remember Social Security. If you do not already get a Social Security Statement every year, you can check your Social Security earnings record by submitting a request form SSA – 7004. The form can be obtained by calling the Social Security Office (1-800-772-1213) or at www.ssa.gov. Your Social Security check can be used to support your retirement.

PLEASE START SAVING TODAY FOR A MORE SECURE FUTURE!

Buying a Home

Are you thinking about buying a home? Buying a home is one of the biggest investments you will ever make! There a few things you need to know before you start looking for a home.

1. Is your credit in good shape – if not, get copies of your credit report from Experian, TransUnion Corporation, and Equifax. The telephone numbers are listed on page 34 of this booklet.

Note: It is better to order a copy from each agency, as they may be slightly different.

2. If there is a problem with your credit rating, get it corrected BEFORE you start looking for a home.

3. Do you make enough money to buy a home?

4. Do you have a 20% down payment?

Note: If there is a problem with any of the areas listed above, get them corrected.

Another important factor in buying a home is the closing costs. The word costs imply many. Closing costs can be as little as several hundred dollars or as much as several thousand dollars, depending on the type of home/property you are buying. Here are some of the terms used in closing costs.

1. Loan Origination Fee – this is probably the most expensive part of the closing costs.

2. Loan Processing Fee – this is the charge for processing your loan paperwork/application.

3. Credit Report Fee – your financial institution runs a credit check on you.

4. Home Inspection Fee – you or your financial institution may ask for an inspection of the property/home to look for needed repairs and how much those repairs may cost before/after the purchase.

5. Property Appraisal Fee – your financial institution will hire a qualified appraiser to make sure the property/home is of proper value for the asking price.

6. Escrow Insurance Fee – this is home insurance monies put into an account that are guaranteed to be paid every month as part of your monthly mortgage payment.

7. Prepaid Interest – this is interest you pay on the loan before closing.

8. Recording Fee – after closing, the deed is recorded at the county court house.

9. Escrow Property Tax – this is property tax monies required by your city/county that are guaranteed to be paid for that year. This money has been divided into 12 monthly payments, collected and held and added to your monthly mortgage payment for payment at the end of the tax year.

10. Legal Fees – these are fees charged by an attorney on your behalf to make sure your rights and interests are protected.

11. Title Insurance – this is property title insurance that protects your investment if for any reason there is a problem with a clear title of the property.

12. Property Survey – this is a survey to show where the boundary markers are located on the property.

Your real estate agent should explain all the closing cost terms with you. If there is anything that you do not understand, do not hesitate to ask! It is very important that you do not sign any document(s) that you do not understand, "ASK/GET HELP!" When you do sign a document, make sure that there are not any blank spaces and that the documents contain everything you agreed too. If not, "ASK/GET HELP!"

Best of luck as you take your journey through the "Steps of Life." Buying a home is a big step in life!

Home Tool Box Checklist

1. Hammer
2. Hand saw
3. Screwdriver set – common
4. Screwdriver set – cross point
5. Electric drill, 3/8 in
6. Tape measure, 12 ft.
7. Extension cord, 25 ft.
8. Safety glasses
9. Step ladder, 6 ft.
10. Pliers, common, 6 in.
11. Pliers, turn off water
12. Wrench, crescent, 6, 8, 10 in.
13. Carpenter level, 24 in.
14. Utility knife

This kit is a basic tool set and is not set in stone. Over time, you will add to it!

Personal Property Inventory

It is very important that you maintain an accurate inventory of all your personal property for insurance purposes, whether you own the home or rent the home. To make an inventory of your personal possessions, go through your home room by room; write down the name and quantity of each item, its date of purchase, and the cost when new and the cost/value now. To determine the current value, check store catalogs and newspapers.

Make and keep separate inventory lists for:

Clothing
Jewelry
Coin Collections
Lawn Equipment (list)
Power Tools (list)
Silverware (list)
Antiques (list)
Furs
Art Works
Stamp Collections
Appliances (list)
Hand Tools (list)
Books
All other possessions

Photograph each room; shoot at different angles to capture the entire rooms' contents. Take close-ups if necessary. Update your inventory annually if necessary. Store the inventory list and photographs in a safe deposit box or other fire proof safety box in the home.

An accurate personal inventory – especially if backed up with photographs can be invaluable in filing an insurance claim if your home or apartment is burglarized, damaged by fire, flood, tornado, or hurricane (if insured). An accurate inventory will also substantiate as "Proof of Loss" to the IRS to claim a tax deduction.

How to Pick a Contractor

1. Determine what is to be done before you call a contractor.

2. Ask your neighbors or friends if they know a good contractor that they would recommend to do the work.

3. Learn the contractor language so will be able to discuss the job with some knowledge.

4. Get estimates in writing from at least three (3) contractors.

5. Check contractor references.

6. Check contractor license with the state, city and/or county. (Ask about complaints.)

7. Call the Better Business Bureau to see if the contractor has had any complaints against his company.

8. Verify that the contractor has workman's compensation and general liability insurance.

9. Ask the contractor how long he has been in business. If he does not have a business address, do not use him.

10. Is the contractor qualified to do the work?

11. Make sure everything you want done is written in the estimate.

12. Make sure all work is guaranteed by the contractor in writing.

13. Never pay for estimates.

14. NEVER pay the contractor in full – payment should be made in increments of onc third now, one third when half of job is completed, and the last third or final payment when work is finished, after your inspection.

15. Never be in a hurry to select a contractor. Always do your homework.

Ordering by Mail

- Never send cash in the mail. Use a check or money order
- Place order at least four weeks before you need the item.
- Check your order for correctness. Be sure you include all shipping and handling charges. (Compare prices with other businesses)
- Insure that your name and address are correct on the order form and on the envelope.
- Keep a complete record of the Seller. Name, address, and phone number of the company. Item ordered, name of the publication where you obtained ad information, and money order or check number.
- The Federal Trade Commission states that after 30 days have elapsed, the company must advise you about the delay and offer you a refund.
- Check to see if satisfaction is guaranteed.
- If you are not satisfied, will the company refund your money and shipping charges?
- Check your order completely when it is received. Notify the company immediately if there is a mistake or damage is discovered.

Note: Make sure damage is noted by delivery person on his copy and your copy of invoice. Have driver sign your copy of invoice.

Wills and Estate

Wills (yours and your wife)

Everyone should have a will – that is if they have anything of value. If you do not have a will when you die, the law of your state will determine what happens to your estate. A will is a legal document in which a person names another person or persons to manage his or her estate upon death. It is best to have an attorney prepare your will, as he will know the laws of your state.

The Personal Affairs Data Worksheet, Cash Flow Statement, and Net Worth Balance Sheet referenced in this booklet will give all necessary information needed to help prepare a will. This information should be kept in a safe place.

Living Will

A living will is a written statement of what kind of medical care you want or do not want if you become unable to make your own decisions. A Living Will is called a "Living Will" because it is only good while you are still living. It is best to have this document prepared by an attorney.

Power of Attorney

A Power of Attorney gives an individual the legal authority to act for another person in legal and business dealings.

About the Author

I was born in Berea of Madison County, Kentucky, June 21, 1927. My parents separated in 1935. My brothers (three) and sisters (three) were sent to various homes. I was sent to Father Flanagan's Boy's Town, in Omaha, Nebraska. I stayed there until 1942 and then returned to Kentucky for a few months. Later, I hitched – hiked to Denver, Colorado where I stayed until 1945. Eventually I was drafted into the U.S. Army. In 1948 I transferred into the U.S. Air Force, where I retired in 1967 as a Technical Sergeant.

My experience and knowledge in writing this booklet comes from:

- Twenty (20) years in the U.S. Army and Air Force
- Ten (10) years working for the U.S. Government in Contract Administration as a Government Property Administrator
- Four (4) years as manager of Central Stores at Eastern Kentucky University
- Four (4) years working with U.S. Government Contractors (classified)

  Air America, Inc
  Thai Airways
  Lao Airways
  Korean Airways
  Continental Airline

- Two (2) years working for Misner Marine Construction Company as a security officer, plant maintenance, and stock identification clerk for all material and equipment returned from offsite construction jobs.

Notes

Notes

CPSIA information can be obtained at www.ICGtesting.com
Printed in the USA
LVOW101456180213

320616LV00016B/882/P

9 781608 62340